EXPERT INTERVIEWS

FOR

EXTRA TRAFFIC

BUILD AUTHORITY TRAFFIC
BY INTERVIEWING SOMEONE IN AUTHORITY

Terms and Conditions

LEGAL NOTICE

The Publisher has strived to be as accurate and complete as possible in the creation of this report, notwithstanding the fact that he does not warrant or represent at any time that the contents within are accurate due to the rapidly changing nature of the Internet.

While all attempts have been made to verify information provided in this publication, the Publisher assumes no responsibility for errors, omissions, or contrary interpretation of the subject matter herein. Any perceived slights of specific persons, peoples, or organizations are unintentional.

In practical advice books, like anything else in life, there are no guarantees of income made. Readers are cautioned to reply on their own judgment about their individual circumstances to act accordingly.

This book is not intended for use as a source of legal, business, accounting or financial advice. All readers are advised to seek services of competent professionals in legal, business, accounting and finance fields.

You are encouraged to print this book for easy reading.

Table Of Contents

Foreword

Expert interview is an innovative way of producing and sharing information. In the ever changing interest and lifestyles of people today there are a lot of different ways of reaching an individual with the intention of sharing information.

Expert Interviews For Extra Traffic

Build authority traffic by interviewing someone in authority

Chapter 1:

Expert Interview Intro

These expert interview scenarios can successfully achieve some percentage of exposure on products, individuals, services and many more. Basically being a series of digitally maneuvered media files that can be done either in the audio or video format, these tools are fast gaining popularity especially for those in the media savvy world.

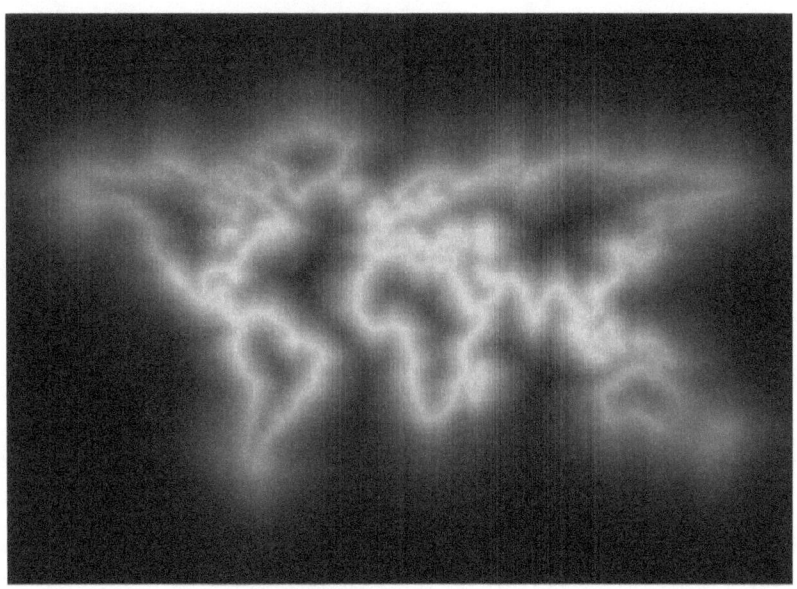

The Basics

These presentations are designed to keep the interest of the viewers in the form of a following as the material is released episodically and downloaded through web syndications.

As most internet marketers are looking for viable tools to add to the enhancement of their business forays the expert interview tool can be useful because of its easy accessibility.

Also the freedom element is certainly a welcome change from other more restrictive tools. Being able to design and feature material that is both flamboyant and unorthodox creates the interest from viewers and others alike. Being a good and accessible tool for promotions and education is also the basis for its popularity.

Exposure is probably the foremost reason this method is chosen and it is effective in being able to achieve this without the need for expert engagement.

While some may consider the expert interview as an inappropriate tool to be used for marketing purposes there are also those that attest to its functionality and effectiveness.

From a sincerity point of view the expert interview tool has the more personal reaching element that can be noted as quite engaging and this of course is a very important feature when trying to use it in the business sense. Also this tool allows for the direct and immediate reaction on the part of the individual privy to the expert interview style.

Chapter 2:

The Benefits Of Expert Interview

Exploring the possible benefits to using the expert interview as a tool for business revenue enhancement is certainly worth the effort. Besides being fairly simple to use this tool has the capability of engaging the potential customer quite effectively.

How It Benefits You

Benefiting from the free download feature is probably the most attractive incentive for making use of this tool. There are no restriction tagged to the download nor are there any pre requirements that need to be met before being able to access the expert interview material.

Another benefit would be that there is no restriction as to the schedules for accessing and using or viewing the expert interview segments.

This is ideal for those busy concentrating on other more pressing matters or simply not interested in viewing the feeds at the moment they are launched.

Being able to design and have creative control over the expert interview content is definitely another benefit when it comes to freedom of ideas and promotional features within the segment.

Making the content outrageously interesting or simply plainly intellectual gives the individual a sense of control and achievement. Should the expert interview be well received and consequently when the services of the individual are sought after revenue can be earned.

If designed well it has another benefit of being used as a great promotional marketing tool and also as a good educational tool. Because of its comparatively cheaper creation costs the expert interview can be used fairly widely and also be able to reach a wider audience base than the more conventional methods can.

The audio and video feature is also another benefit when it comes to reaching the younger audience. Proven to being more effective in engaging the attention of the younger audience the expert interview has been able to benefit its users consistently and successfully.

Chapter 3:

How To Use Expert Interview Correctly

Using the expert interview tool for enhancing the business possibilities effectively the individual must be aware that reaching the customer at different varying levels is the goal.

How To Use It

Filling the customer funnel, path or interest basically consists of three major parts which are pre purchase, purchase and post purchase. Thus choosing the expert interview tool would effectively be able to address all three aspects adequately.

The effectiveness of any marketing campaign is to stay away from any tool that claims to cater to and suit everyone's needs in one package. However expert interview can actually make this claim without any adverse repercussions.

The sincerity and integrity of the style and content can be designed to suit or cater to any section of different target audiences effectively and quickly.

The perceived transparency and authenticity of the expert interview tool further contributes to the effectiveness of reaching the target audience and perhaps maybe even those who are not directly interested or connected to the content, product, or service.

The expert interview tool can be effectively used when information exchanged has the opportunity to be challenged and the possible rebuttals are immediately available for anyone to view. This is also effective in creating an instant platform for all queries to be adequately addressed and answered.

The expert interview platform can also be effectively used to disseminate as much information as possible without actually having to spend too much time on technicalities thus providing the viewer with easily understood material.

The probing style of this tool also effectively creates a certain level of discernment when the viewer is considering a purchase of the product, service or even when the viewer is considering making a recommendation.

Another reason the expert interview style has proven effective is because of its simplicity element. The directness of getting and giving information is clearly defined in the style of delivery chosen. Viewers can then instantly conclude or form an opinion of the content and then decide the next course of action on their part.

Chapter 4:

Making Money With Expert Interview

There are several reason for expert interview to be successfully used as a money making tool. Some of which are fairly common while others may have some newer connotations attached to it.

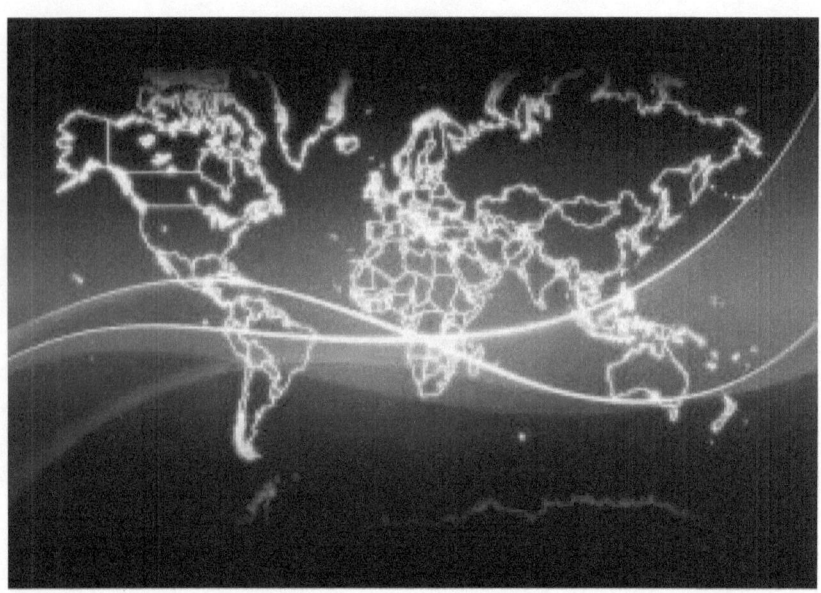

Bringing In The Cash

The expert interview tool is primarily a tool that is used to address a target audience. This target audience can then be turned into a money making possibility, this is because of the advertisements that can be tagged to the interview session to bring in added revenue.

There are interested parties who specifically look for expert interview platforms that have a very good following of target audiences and then proceed to offer remuneration of adds posted within the interview frame or even as promotional or budget incentives. There is also the possibility of being able to make money through the ability to attract sponsors.

Giving away some things for free when a purchase has been confirmed is also another way of earning money through these expert interview platforms.

When the customer is already keen on making a purchase based on the information given the added feature of give aways will only serve to delight the customers and creating the possibility of consequent visit or even referrals.

Another way of garnering possible revenue is to use teasers or only show partial expert interview for free and then charge a small fee to view the rest. However the teaser or partial content available for viewing must be attractive enough to encourage the viewer to want to complete the viewing even if it is at as cost.

Building media network based on expert interview and then selling advertising space is also another way to gain revenue. This can be quite lucrative especially if the sight has a consistently huge target audience.

Therefore with some research done into what can be interesting for viewers the general content can be designed and produced to ensure definite interest from viewers.

Chapter 5:

Writing A Book With Expert Interview

Among the simplest formulas for how to compose a book is to question experts in your niche or industry and produce the book. And as simple as this is to do right, it's simple to "mess up" too. So let me demonstrate how to produce an interview book in a way that it really drives individuals back to you and your business.

Authoring

Simply record interviews with experts or industry leadership and turn those interviews into chapters of your book.

I've witnessed interview books work well and I've seen them read like last year's news. So prior to you grabbing your voice recorder and running off to talk to individuals, let me help you prevent making huge errors.

Huge error #1: No goal other than to slap a book together

Don't simply decide that you ought to compose a book and a series of conversations. You have to produce something of value that individuals wish to read or there's no point composing the book. So determine a particular result for the reader. What's in it for them?

Huge error #2: Lack of clearness for how the book benefits both you and your subscriber

If you don't know precisely where you're taking the reader with these interviews and how the book will locate you as the go-to authority, you'll compose a namby-pamby book that does little if anything for you as an authority and business owner and simply less for the reader.

Huge error #3: hapless choice of experts

You can't simply interview somebody merely as they "do the correct thing" or bear the correct sort of business. If you do, you're likely to have a difficult time assembling a book individuals wish to read.

Huge error #4: Failing to design your interviews

You can't simply turn on a voice recorder and have your interviewee begin speaking. You either require a set of questions you ask each authority or a particular set designed to bring out the brilliance of the particular individual you're interviewing.

Huge error #5: No overarching message or topic

You wish more than a set of chats put on paper (or into ebooks). Every chapter, and thus every interview, has to in some way move forward the book's message.

Huge error #6: putting in nothing to the interviews

I don't know how come, but individuals who compose this sort of book tend to simply turn transcripts into chapters and add nothing at all to them. If you do this, you're not aligning yourself as the authority and not adding to your own report.

Now that I've soundly rained on your parade, let me demonstrate how to produce an interview book that really establishes you as an industry leader worth listening to.

How to compose the interview books

Measure 1: forge the flow (or outline or contents) of the book.

Choose what you wish each chapter to say based on your designated outcome. Your book isn't at the whim of your interviewees. It's up to you to determine it.

Measure 2: pick out the experts that equate to your chapters.

When you understand what has to be in your book, contact the best industry leadership who fit this profile. It's crucial to select your experts well. Select them as they've a unique spin, a specialty, a strong story or another element that adds to the advantage of your book.

Measure 3: produce your list of questions that you'll ask everyone.

This will provide you an overall structure for every interview that will produce a book that makes common sense to the reader. Allow room for 2 or 3 that are particular to each interviewee so you may showcase their brilliance.

Measure 4: Once you've your list of interviewees, arrange your schedule and get busy.

Add. 2-3 narrowed down questions you'll ask your experts based on what you understand about them particularly. Make sure to make 2 recordings so you have a backup.

Measure 5: put together your book.

Make transcripts of the interviews. Why not add some of your own personality and expertness to each chapter? You may merely add an introduction and a conclusion with some of your own thoughts.

After finishing these steps, you have your interview book. If you've put in your own thoughts, your book demonstrates your expertise instead of only adding to the great name of your interviewees. You may be proud of this book that boosts your business.

Chapter 6:

What To Avoid

As most interesting expert interview sessions are either audio or visual, the quality of the production is quite important. Poorly produced work will not be able to stay competitive and garner the desired target audience. Therefore avoid substandard work.

What To Stay Away From

Equipment used should also be able to successfully create a good piece of quality work. Avoid using computer or webcam microphones when trying to keep cost down in doing an expert interview. Some costs are just not stinging on. If the audio quality is poor the target audience will not be able to enjoy or focus on the message, thus causing the quick loss of interest.

Though having a general script to follow, diligently keeping to the script would not allow the freedom of the parties involved to express what they need to and thus giving the target audience a rather bland experience. Avoid the insincerity of prepared scripts because as a marketing tool the customer will definitely not feel comfortable nor be adequately convinced to make a purchase.

Avoid length expert interview sessions. Even if the product, service, or material being featured is very interesting, designing a long drawn session will only end up working adversely towards the promotion of the content. Also designing the content to consist of too much technical information should be avoided. Most viewers are not really interested in the technical aspects of anything and would rather just know how the item can benefit them. Furthermore those who require more technical information will be more willing to seek the information needed.

Wrapping Up

When time and money is a dominating factor in the daily routine of an individual, the element of wasting either is avoided at all costs. Therefore in order to get and hold the attention of an individual long enough to ensure the general context of the expert interview has been understood, some things needs to be seriously avoided. Hopefully this book has given you some insight into what is needed to use this technique of marketing.